TRUTHS in VERSE

C.M. Masner

Praise for *Poetic Theft*

Charles Masner's *Poetic Theft* takes on the perennial subjects of poetry: beginnings and endings, love and death, beauty and war. From short, pithy poems to longer prose pieces, Masner confronts life's biggest questions with wit, grace, and unflinching emotional directness. "You must remember the moon," he writes, "because the moon will not remember you." *Poetic Theft* is a lively, generous book.

- John Brehm, author of *Help Is on the Way*,
winner of the 2012 Four Lakes Prize

Masner is a writer of mystery and of vitality. Curious about the world, he looks for words that might authentically capture pieces of it: "There must be some word for stars. / Some word other than diamonds." Accordingly, this ambitious collection of poetry and prose runs the gamut from busted marriages to redemptive seductions, from car wrecks to summer dresses, from weddings to whiskey, from burger joints to hospitals, always attentive to love and sorrow. Masner presents these scenes of his own life and the lives of others and thereby conjures a rich, full creation.

- David J. Rothman, former Resident Poet,
Colorado Public Radio

Edited by Leeanne Seaver

Book Design by Alyssa Ohnmacht

Cover Photos: C.M. Masner

Readers: Abby Dollarhide and Isaac Duncan

ISBN 978-0-578-74717-0

for Emily

who wrote words in poetic line
and who told the Truth – slant, with rhyme

TABLE OF CONTENTS

INTRODUCTION

As a poet, Ernest Hemingway was a great novelist. Well, I think he was pretty good, but I don't write the canon. Here are some words Mr. Hemingway wrote:

> In the late summer of that year we lived in a house in a village that looked across the river and the plain to the mountains. In the bed of the river there were pebbles and boulders, dry and white in the sun, and the water was clear and swiftly moving and blue in the channels. Troops went by the house and down the road and the dust they raised powdered the leaves of the trees. The trunks of the trees too were dusty and the leaves fell early that year and we saw the troops marching along the road and the dust rising and leaves, stirred by the breeze, falling and the soldiers marching and afterward the road bare and white except for the leaves.

This is the first paragraph of *A Farewell to Arms.*

Here is some more writing I like:

> As the herd moved it became a carpet of rust-brown and grey and dull red. It was not like a herd of cattle or of sheep, because it was wild, and it carried with it the stamp of wilderness and the freedom of a land still more a possession of Nature than of men. To see ten thousand animals untamed and not branded with the symbols of human commerce is like scaling an unconquered mountain for the first time, or like finding a forest without roads or footpaths, or the blemish of an axe. You know then what you had always been told—that the world once lived and grew without adding machines and newsprint and brick-walled streets and the tyranny of clocks.

This is from Beryl Markham's memoir, *West with the Night,* about which Hemingway wrote, "[S]he has written so well, and marvelously well, that I was completely ashamed of myself as a writer."

And one more:

> In the waste fields strung with barbed wire where the thistles grow over hidden minefields there exists a curious freedom. Between the guns of the deployed powers, between the march of patrols and policing dogs there is an uncultivated strip of land from which law and man himself have retreated. Along this uneasy border the old life has come back into its own. Weeds grow and animals slip about in the night where no man dares to hunt them. A thin uncertain line fringes the edge of oppression. The freedom it contains is fit only for birds and floating thistledown or a wandering fox. Nevertheless, there must be men who look upon it with envy.

This is the first paragraph, of the first essay, in Loren Eiseley's book of essays, *The Night Country*.

Let us continue to set the table—a metaphor in progress:

> Because I could not stop for Death –
> He kindly stopped for me –
> The Carriage held but just Ourselves –
> And Immortality.
>
> - Emily Dickinson

"Nothing Gold Can Stay"

> Nature's first green is gold,
> Her hardest hue to hold.
> Her early leaf's a flower;
> But only so an hour.
> Then leaf subsides to leaf.
> So Eden sank to grief.
> So dawn goes down to day.
> Nothing gold can stay.
>
> - Robert Frost

"When I Heard the Learn'd Astronomer"

> When I heard the learn'd astronomer,
> When the proofs, the figures, were ranged in columns
>   before me,

When I was shown the charts and diagrams, to add, divide,
    and measure them,
When I sitting heard the astronomer where he lectured with
    much applause in the lecture-room,
How soon unaccountable I became tired and sick,
Till rising and gliding out I wander'd off by myself,
In the mystical moist night-air, and from time to time,
Look'd up in perfect silence at the stars.

                                - Walt Whitman

     Whatever one thinks of the artistic merit of the writings of Mr. Hemingway, Ms. Markham, and Professor Eiseley, reasonable people will agree that all of the writings I have provided are paragraphs, composed of sentences. They are prose, although tidy paragraphs and sentences are not always necessary for a piece of writing to be called prose, or, more obviously, poetry. James Joyce, for example. The concluding lines of *Ulysses*. The sentence that ends in the period ends a section of not quite fifty pages, with but one other period, and a few breaks that might be called paragraphs.

    . . . O and the sea the sea crimson sometimes like fire and the
glorious sunsets and the figtrees in the Alameda gardens yes and
all the queer little streets and pink and blue and yellow houses and
the rosegardens and the jessamine and geraniums and cactuses and
Gibraltar as a girl where I was a flower of the mountain yes when I
put the rose in my hair like the Andalusian girls used or shall I wear
a red yes and how he kissed me under the Moorish wall and I
thought well as well him as another and then I asked him with my
eyes to ask again yes and then he asked me would I yes to say yes
my mountain flower and first I put my arms around him yes and
drew him down to me so he could feel my breasts all perfume yes
and his heart was going like mad and yes I said yes I will Yes.

    Can we call the prose pieces *prose poems?* I have no objection, but if you demur, can we at least call them *poetical?* Is there not a cadence to the progression of the language? Some repetition of sound? Some appeal to emotion? Are not these "poetical" qualities? Are they not qualities found in the poems of Ms. Dickinson, Mr. Frost, and Mr. Whitman?

    And now we come to my confession, my argument, the room for disagreement. Some may argue that neither good prose nor good poetry require the qualities I have described. Rhythm, a repetition of sounds, an appeal to emotion.

Perhaps this is true for certain types of scientific or legal writing, although, even here, I think there is room for debate. But in fiction, in poetry, and in creative non-fiction, as in music and all other art, I believe these qualities to be essential, although they can be present in varying degrees. In the visual arts, without sound, the sights alone become the sounds; rhythm the composition of the sights. In the visual arts, such as dance, the rhythm is a composition of both sights and sound. Of course, the rhythms, the sounds, the appeals to emotion, can run the gamut from shallow to profound. That's why we have readers and critics. In any case, however, no one finds it to be a compliment to have one's poetry, or one's prose, called *prosaic*.

Verse forms, such as the sonnet among others I have included in this collection of poems, are but the most historically well-known and well-organized word constructions of rhythm and sounds that appeal to our emotions through language. I chose to write in the particular forms in this collection because for one reason or another the form appealed to me, and I thought I could write something worthy of the form.

Certain verse forms, such as the sonnet, have gotten a bad rap because they have been determined to be the hegemonic progeny of DWGs (dead white guys). I am not convinced that there is anything culturally confining about such verse forms, except to the extent that all form is, by definition, confining and hierarchical. Even air has a form and a hierarchy, although its chemical formula will vary. Hierarchy of some kind is inherent and inevitable in the world. Anarchy can become something democratic or tyrannical, but it will evolve. I do understand, however, that it could be harder to like a sonnet if it had been invented by Adolph Hitler.

In 1984, Audre Lorde presented her essay of protest on the lack of representation of black lesbian feminists and poor women at a feminist conference attended mostly by white feminists. The title of Ms. Lorde's essay is, *The Master's Tools Will Never Dismantle the Master's House*. In a central paragraph of her essay, Ms. Lorde wrote:

> Those of us who stand outside the circle of this society's definition of acceptable women; those of us who have been forged in the crucibles of difference—those of us who are poor, who are lesbians, who are Black, who are older—know that survival is not an academic skill. It is learning how to take our differences and make them strengths. For the master's tools will never dismantle the master's house. They may allow us temporarily to beat him at his

own game, but they will never enable us to bring about genuine change. And this fact is only threatening to those women who still define the master's house as their only source of support.

Ms. Lorde concluded her essay with a quote from Aimè Cèsaire's play, *A Tempest,* adapted from Shakespeare's play, *The Tempest.* Caliban is speaking.

> Prospero, you are the master of illusion.
> Lying is your trademark.
> And you have lied so much to me
> (Lied about the world, lied about me)
> That you have ended by imposing on me
> An image of myself.
> Underdeveloped, you brand me, inferior,
> That is the way you have forced me to see myself
> I detest that image! What's more, it's a lie!
> But now I know you, you old cancer,
> And I know myself as well.[1]

Words are the life of crime, and words are the life of freedom. And the arts of the heart make the human animal more than animal.

C.M. Masner

---

[1] I found this Cèsaire quote included, as a conclusion, in an online reprint of Ms. Lorde's essay. I did not find it included as a conclusion in the book of Ms. Lorde's essays I have listed as a reference.

WORKS CITED

Cèsaire, Aimè. *A Tempest*. New York: Theater Communications Group, Inc. 1985, 1992 English translations by Richard Miller. French copyright 1969.

Dickinson, Emily. *Final Harvest, Poem #290 (Poem # 712 in The Complete Poems of Emily Dickinson)*. New York: Little, Brown and Company, 1962. I have quoted the first four-line stanza of Ms. Dickinson's six four-line stanza poem.

Eiseley, Loren. *The Night Country*. "The Gold Wheel." Lincoln, NE: University of Nebraska Press, 1997. Reprinted from the original 1971 edition by Charles Scribner's Sons, An Imprint of Simon & Schuster Inc., New York.

Frost, Robert. *The Robert Frost Reader,* edited by Edward Connery Lathem and Lawrence Thompson. "Nothing Gold Can Stay." New York: Holt, Rinehart and Winston, 1972.

Hemingway, Ernest. *A Farewell To Arms*. New York: Charles Scribner's Sons, 1929. (I like The Hemingway Library Edition.)

Joyce, James. *Ulysses*. New York: First Vintage International Edition, 1990.

Lorde, Audre. *The Master's Tools Will Never Dismantle the Master's House.* 1984. *Sister Outsider: Essays and Speeches*, Ed. Berkeley, CA: Crossing Press. 110-114. 2007.

Markham, Beryl. *West With The Night*. Berkeley, CA: North Point Press. 1983. Reprinted from the original 1942 edition by Houghton Mifflin Company, Boston, MA.

Whitman, Walt. *Leaves of Grass,* 1855, in *The Portable Walt Whitman*. London, England: Penguin Group, 2004. Warner, Michael, editor. "When I Heard the Learn'd Astronomer."

POEMS

The Ballad of Billy and Carrie Anne

Sweet Billy was a little slow,
but he loved Carrie Anne.
And Carrie Anne was slower still,
but Billy was her friend.

Oh Billy, sweet blue-eyed Billy,
Billy loved Carrie Anne.
Oh Billy, sweet blue-eyed Billy,
loved brown-eyed Carrie Anne.

Billy's face was all pimpled full.
His teeth a crooked brown.
But Billy was a gentle soul.
Loved every child in town.

Carrie Anne's hair was wheat gold blonde.
Her face was blemish free.
Her fairest skin was newborn soft.
As all the boys could see.

Two men with names of Jake and Jim,
came round to Carrie Anne.
Tried to take what she would not give,
to prove that they were men.

Billy stopped those men, Jake and Jim.
And could have hurt them bad.
Instead he let them run from him,
with all the hate they had.

Carrie Anne loved her sweet Billy.
Billy loved Carrie Anne.
And of that love a son was born.
He was their little man.

Little Billy was handsome bright.
His mother's loving joy.
No fairer child of day or night,
than blue-eyed Billy boy.

Then Jake and Jim came round with hate.
Came round with hate again.
With loaded guns they lay in wait.
Murder would be their sin.

Jake and Jim killed blue-eyed Billy.
And both got time for life.
Carrie Anne lost blue-eyed Billy,
now brown-eyed widow wife.

Oh Billy, sweet blue-eyed Billy,
Billy loved Carrie Anne.
Oh Billy, sweet blue-eyed Billy,
loved brown-eyed Carrie Anne.

Now old heart brown-eyed Carrie Anne.
Long gone blue-eyed lover.
And her blue-eyed son grew a man,
each day mother's treasure.

Love's the moral of this story.
We all die, in the end.
Love is all of God and glory.
Love, love, and love again.

Oh Billy, sweet blue-eyed Billy,
Billy loves Carrie Anne.
Oh Billy, sweet blue-eyed Billy,
loves brown-eyed Carrie Anne.

It's Always Something

"It's always something" – he used to say – come what may.
And I have to admit – that's always been true.
It was true on the birth of his very first day.
Something – whether nighttime born, or after morning dew.
Something, some things, this child never knew.
A well-fed belly along childhood's way.
Some store-bought clothes, washed and new.
Something from nothing is hard they say.

A regular bath to wash the stink away.
A little affection to kiss his heart when blue.
A daddy who had less for drink, and more for pay.
A road less rocky from the hole in your shoe.
It's easy to love dollars, when the pennies are few.
The poor are preached work, the rich get to play.
The rich look happy, from the poor man's pew.
Something from nothing is hard they say.

And where is this God his mind can't pray?
This something God who said – "You're through."
Are we created in God's image for prey?
Or is God just a being we demented too?
What's real is gone – but the body's still on view.
Life is hard served pills on a tray.
But, dear God, who cares, if it's not you?
Something from nothing is hard they say.

Envoi

Prince, God, Holy Spirit – one, three, or two –
His pain, my pain, our pain – at your feet we lay.
I just wish there was something you could do.
Something from nothing is hard they say.

The Patriarchal Blues

The blues be the worst man I ever had.
The blues be the worst man I ever had.
I make a man happy, when he be sad.

The blues be the best man I ever had.
The blues be the best man I ever had.
I make a man happy, when he be sad.

The blues the only man I ever had.
The blues the only man I ever had.
I make a man happy, when he be sad.

Grrlfriend, the blues be your man I just had.
Grrlfriend, the blues be your man I just had.
Grrlfriend, make him happy, or you be sad.
Grrlfriend, make him happy, or you be sad.

It Was Her Fiddle Made Me Sing

I held her close and loved her well.
And then she asked me not to tell.
I said my sweet I'll say no word.
But now, of course, you all have heard.
I am just a bow made of string.
It was her fiddle made me sing.
Or, violin, if you prefer.
I mean no disrespect to her.
Either way, she's a work of art.
All I did was to play my part.

The Romantic Cowboy

I touch the western breeze in song.
I see the snow freeze rocky mountain.
I know that land is right and wrong.
I know that death is weak and strong.
Mountains die and rivers fountain.
I ride the plains from east to west.
I ride the plains from south to north.
And reach the place I love the best.
A lonesome heart my song breaks forth.
Until death's valley takes my rest.

A Ghazal for Beauty

I must go back briefly to a place I have loved
to tell you those you will efface I have loved.

~ Agha Shahid Ali, "I Have Loved"
from *Call Me Ishmael Tonight*

I remember the sound of "Amazing Grace."
In the divine of music, I found beauty.

I saw her dark gaze meant not for me.
In the eyes of angels, I found beauty.

The web spun a home in the careless wind.
In the black, and red, and blue of the spider, I found beauty.

There was an old tree, knarled and spent.
In the forests of the land, I found beauty.

There was a path I once chose to take.
In the trails of the land, I found beauty.

The taste of the beer was a summer night.
In the taverns of the town, I found beauty.

The pearls were left to rest on the corner of the bed.
In the jewels of the world, I found beauty.

It was a weed with spines brown like my prick.
In the gardens of the world, I found beauty.

The mushroom decayed in a reddish brown.
In the soiled of the world, I found beauty.

The bark of the tree was chafed like old skin.
In the old trees of the world, I found beauty.

Light through windows made shadows from shine.
In the shadowed lights of the world, I found beauty.

The old building stood silver against the moon.
In the nights of the world, I found beauty.

The trees in the forest waved leaves at me.
In the branches of the world, I found beauty.

The staircase led to a private place.
In the lonely of the world, I found beauty.

The rocks were washed in the water of rain.
In the wash of the world, I found beauty.

The sunset red over the rooftop of home.
In the settling suns of the world, I found beauty.

The boardwalk shared the bank of the lake.
In the shared of the world, I found beauty.

The buzzard roosted on the ledge of the dam.
In the scavenge of the world, I found beauty.

The ducks took a walk down to the water.
In the flights of the world, I found beauty.

There was wine and cheese on a creekside table.
In the small blessings of the world, I found beauty.

The steeple rose to meet the sky.
In the chapels of mortals, I found beauty.

A bee and a flower mated.
In the couples of the world, I found beauty.

The land was there to meet the sky.
In the meetings of the world, I found beauty.

Girls in dresses on bicycles rode by.
Inside the dresses of the world, I found beauty.

There were cottage houses in the town.
In the shared spaces of the world, I found beauty.

I saw a deer on the trail.
In unknown friends on trails, I found beauty.

I saw a turtle on the trail.
Inside the shelled hearts of the world, I found beauty.

I saw a snake just skinned on the trail.
In God's fallen angel, I found beauty.

The butterfly fluttered wings to dry.
In the cocoons of the world, I found beauty.

I saw two lovers before he broke her heart.
In the dreams of the world, I found beauty.

I saw an old bridge I had to cross.
In the crossings of the world, I found beauty.

I saw a lover die after she kissed me.
In the death of pain, I found beauty.

I saw a rainbow color the sky.
In the lights of the world, I found beauty.

I heard chimes in the wind.
In the winds of the world, I found beauty.

I saw her from the side she could not see.
In the blind sides of the world, I found beauty.

A flower grows from a crack in the wall.
In the broken of the world, I found beauty.

I saw pictures of the dead.
In the memories of the world, I found beauty.

I saw train tracks run out of my sight.
In the journeys of the world, I found beauty.

I dreamed of snowflakes on a warm summer night.
In the imaginations of the world, I found beauty.

There was pain and death all over the world.
And since there was no God, I found beauty.

Hillbilly Seduction

A fall time Ozarks.
With spring and summer sweet wines.
Then winter – she's mine.

body and soul

i want to rock and roll your soul
till your heart gets hot
for what i got
i want you to have all i have
till i have not

i need to rock and roll your soul
till your heart gets caught
by what i got
i need you to have all i have
till i have not

i love to rock and roll your soul
till your heart gets taught
by what i got
i love when you have all i have
and i have not

hot, caught, and taught
baby – i want ever thing you got

He Could Not Conquer All

I saw him move through space and time.
His gaited pace so much like mine.
But I was no more young and small.
Who knew he could not conquer all?

Why do we live and then must die?
He did not choose from grace to fall.
Who makes the tears we use to cry?
Who knew he could not conquer all?

His last breath he made ours to call.
Who knew he could not conquer all?

The staff all waited in the hall.
Who knew he could not conquer all?

Mortal Gods

"...we only get to vanish once..."

Chris Ransick, from *A Good Man Goes Down*

We want to make a rhyme of death.
And make the rhyme worth all our breath.
We want the rhyme forever heard.
We – the mortal Gods of word.

We want our loves to live again.
We want their voices to be heard.
We want the truth to win again.
We – the mortal Gods of word.

Immortal Gods can never die.
But can their hearts still laugh and cry?
We sing the song of the mockingbird.
We – the mortal Gods of word.

Hopeless Romantics Confront Death

They think about beauty.
And then they think some more of truth.
Then they think about love.
Three mysteries of time and space.
No proportion – no grace.
And for poetry – God's duty.

Soldier of the Cross

I thought about the war.
And then I thought some more of death.
Doubt's faith ends with death's breath.
Is it God who giveth this much?
God's cursed human touch?

Heaven's cross: made grave's crutch: once more.

Red Bike Girls

A blue dressed girl on a red bike rode by.
Her young legs leaned into the summer wind.
The summer wind caressed her legs thigh high.
And I wondered just how her day would end.
A girl of twenty she seemed to my eye.
How many heartbreaks had she known by then?
So much depends upon these red bike girls.
In summer blue dresses the wind unfurls.

The Real Is What You Feel

Romantic poetry is such a bore.
All those flowers and pitiful stuff.
I want reality, and nothing more.
Poetry needs a lot less stuffy fluff.
The world is full of blood and guts and gore.
We need less tender, and a lot more tough.
But, alas, all I do is sit and cry.
My sweet flower just kissed my ass goodbye.

Angels of the Heart

A human life is a work of art: this is always the ideal.
This is what a better angel taught me.
A darker angel taught me a hunger I had to heal.
A better angel and a darker angel are how I came to be.

This is what a better angel taught me.
A better angel taught me that paradox is the master of the heart.
A better angel and a darker angel are how I came to be.
A darker angel taught me that death was the hardest part.

A better angel taught me that paradox is the master of the heart.
A darker angel taught me a hunger I had to heal.
A darker angel taught me that death was the hardest part.
A human life is a work of art: this is always the ideal.

The Solo's Part

If this be God's plan, then how can God be?
God took the sorrows he can take from you.
God took your sorrows and gave them to me.
The sorrows of love are now one, not two.

God took the sorrows he can take from you.
Who takes the sorrows from my broken heart?
The sorrows of love are now one, not two.
Who teaches me to sing the solo's part?

Who takes the sorrows from my broken heart?
God took your sorrows and gave them to me.
Who teaches me to sing the solo's part?
If this be God's plan, then how can God be?

Nightshade Heart

The sunlight looks for shadows to compare.
But darkness finds you hidden and shade free.
The darkness finds you far away from me.
Yet still I taste the scent of nightshade air.

I thought, my love, I held you kind and fair.
I thought, my love, that you loved me truly.
I thought, my love, that you and I were we.
There were no secrets for us not to share.

It was too close for us to be, dear heart.
I see that now in all my solitude.
It was destined that we two should depart.
It was destined you were cherried tart.
I see that now as I hum a sad etude.
It's life for me, and hell for you, sweetheart.

Nightshade Lover

The sunlight looks for shadows to compare.
But darkness finds you hidden and shade free.
The darkness finds you far away from me.
Yet still I taste the scent of nightshade air.

I thought, my love, I held you kind and fair.
I thought, my love, that you loved me truly.
I thought, my love, that you and I were we.
There were no secrets for us not to share.

It was too close for us to be, lover.
I see that now in all my solitude.
It was destined that we two should depart.
It was destined you be Eden's flower.
I see that now as I hum a sad etude.
It's life for me, and hell for you, sweetheart.

Rhyme Royal without Apology

Dark powers there be in today's poetry.
These powers opine no rhyme should be penned.
No rhyme from begin to end should we see.
No rhymes and no lines that stop at the end.
So say these powers that be, my good friend.
But the songs of the world are rhymes in verse.
I'll sing songs – they can listen up the arse.

Truths in Verse

What would we be, without God's mystery?
If God is great, can God bring death to time?
What would God be, without our history?
If God is great, why does the world have crime?
If God is great, can God write poems that rhyme?
I sometimes think God goes from bad to worse.
Let's help ourselves, and write our truths in verse.

When the Sad Song Plays

When the sad song plays on the radio,
back in the day where all lovers go,
where mystery cries in the night,
and hearts break for morning light.
Romance is a dance that dreamers know.

Our hearts break and broke so full of woe.
You my Juliet, and I your Romeo.
It was and is so wrong and oh so right –
                    When the sad song plays.

Twilight is a time the poets like to crow.
A time when beauty means more than show.
A time when death is both dark and bright.
Something's lost and something's found for hearts that break at such a sight.
Yeah, you know she's crazy, when she gets that glow.
                    When the sad song plays.

Mystery

Mystery is the life of death – it came from the life of man to be.
Truth for would-be poets and philosophers to share.
In heaven can there be a place to be free?
High forever is low for never – so who would care?

I know there are those who think me unfair.
Those who long so much for eternity.
But there are vows to be made to a God more, or less, rare.
Mystery is the life of death – it came from the life of man to be.

Prayer is the plea we make for immortality.
Sweet hour of prayer, sweet hour of prayer.
A romantic's heart is a fool for the mystery of divinity.
Truth for would-be poets and philosophers to share.

True believers call it the greatest story ever told – and they try to tell it everywhere.
But it was told by men still here – not yet crossed over that final Jordan sea.
How do we know they're all happy – "up there"?
In heaven can there be a place to be free?

I think God has a lot to explain to you and me.
I think God needs at least some of our burdens to bear.
And will heaven be the end for poetry?
High forever is low for never – so who would care?
                    Mystery is the life of death.

December Memory

Don't forget to remember, was the after whisper of her sugar glow.
    I had her for English my freshmen year, first home away
        September.
I was eighteen years old from a southern town where she'd never go.
    Don't forget to remember.

She taught me the ways from May to December.
    She taught me the how of the making of love made real
        slow.
She taught me to conquer required a surrender.

She taught me love words from books shelved for show.
    Her ebony skin made the words tinder, and ember, and even more tender.
So I sent her the flowers I could never send her
    with words she would have wanted to know.
    Don't forget to remember.

We had words

We had words, my heart bled – a few last words from me.
　　　I wrote him last words in papers he read.
I wrote him last words he would never see.
　　　We had words, my heart bled.

Blue eyes, blue casket – mother chose his cemetery bed.
　　　His grave a shadow – in the light of his friends and family.
His four sons spoke of their father – their father now dead.

There's no way to sum our eternity.
　　　If there be a God, God speaks words unsaid.
I wrote my father's obituary.
　　　We had words, my heart bled.

A Lover's Questions - for Rhonda

What makes a love poem song to sing?
What makes a love song poem to say?
Questions I've been contemplating.
I think about them night and day.
Hey baby, love is everything.
Teach me the words I need to play.

How to capture my heart beating?
How to steal your sweet heart away?
Need of you is more than fleeting.
December wants to marry May.
Hey baby, love is everything.
Teach me the words I need to play.

Let's quit this sugar daddy thing.
I want more than a Rhonda lay.
Let's make this bling a diamond ring.
I promise you I'll never stray.
Hey baby, love is everything.
Teach me the words I need to play.

Sweetheart, you're the beauty of spring.
I'm distinguished and Grecianed gray.
All I know to you I can bring.
But I don't have your M.F.A.
Hey baby, love is everything.
Teach me the words I need to play.

Sweet Young Thing

There's mystery to ev'ry thing.
That's what the philosophers say.
Why must we love so much the spring?
And not the winter skies of grey?
My first love was a sweet young thing.
She was a flower bloomed in May.

Her rapture was my heart beating.
I craved her touch, in ev'ry way.
Sweet lullabies her voice did sing.
Her sweet breasts my lips begged to stay.
My first love was a sweet young thing.
She was a flower bloomed in May.

But our love was made for parting.
I grew older and then I strayed.
All first loves must have their ending.
All hearts must break and die someday.
My first love was a sweet young thing.
She was a flower bloomed in May.

Youth and beauty, both are fleeting.
That's what the philosophers say.
But their touch our hearts keep seeking.
The lover's touch that makes us pray.
My first love was a sweet young thing.
She was a flower bloomed in May.

A Lover's Confession

For love, I prayed.
There was no God could be my King.
For love, I prayed.
No holy words to end my day.
I told my lover ev'ry thing.
I knew her heart was listening.
For love, I prayed.

A Plea for Beauty

Slave and Master of the heart, hear our plea.
Prize the dream till might is right.
Slave and Master of the heart, hear our plea.
A dream of sea to shining sea.
Crimson, golden, brown, black, and white.
Our Beauty depends on Liberty's light.
Slave and Master of the heart, hear our plea.

Sioux Goddess

Sioux Goddess has green eyes and black silk hair.
Turquoise is the color of the jewels she likes to wear.
I wonder what long lost Brave was her Chief.
The tattoos I can see are feathers she's laid bare.

I know she needs no Chief to make her brave.
The proud Chiefs are long ago gone to the grave.
Those who rocked their cradles are long gone away.
All those proud races could not make of land a slave.

It was ordained by those who could plot and plow.
And what could have been another way, and how?
If land is meant for fox, and buffalo, and beauty to roam?
How do you teach a free born people your word is not your vow?

Tribal lands were reserved for our native ancestors.
But most of the best went to the farmers, the ranchers, the settlers.
Sioux Goddess dreams of an ancient pride.
And grows rich from the accounts of the callers she favors.

Slaves and Sharecroppers

Nostalgia is a cloak of lies you wear.
It wears better when I am never there.
White privilege don't make my car payments.
Whitey, you are priv'leged everywhere.

Your Southern white mommas gave me the tease.
Your Southern white daddies hung me from trees.
Them poor sharecropper sins ain't mine to own.
My mommas were raped, and made to beg please.

You've never been other so you don't know.
You've got white power wherever you go.
No one can choose the world they were born.
I want the good book to reap what I sow.

None of us others are goin' away.
Not until death or the last judgment day.
I just want all of us to get along.
That's what all you white crackers like to say.

We all pray for a better land on high.
We all sing songs of a sweet bye and bye.
We have the same God from cradle to grave.
There is no God who has told a white lie.

A Sestina for My Love

The spring snow falls on the mountain wood.
In our bed I feel the soft touch of you warmed by me.
I am in need of you when the light falls in the night.
I want you in the break light of every morn.
The sun always shines again I know.
It turns the snow into the river flow of spring.

I remember our bed of winter as it becomes a spring.
The smell of pines and your perfume of sandalwood.
These are memories that lovers know.
There is no pleasure you do not provide me.
Your sighs and moans in our love break of the morn.
The wet sex of the morning on sheets wet from the night.

I wonder how those you made blind recovered from so black a night.
The memories of other lovers and winters turned from spring.
I kill the thought of them when I take you in the break of morn.
The taste of your kisses on other lips becomes the taste of wormwood.
The hearts you broke to free yourself for me.
These are memories I can never know.

I have thought of other lovers you do not know.
You take the past of me in the morn, and in the night.
I know you know there is a past of me.
I have thought of other winters turned to spring.
I have thought of other scents from other heartwood.
I have thought of other lovers I have loved in the morn.

We became in love in the morn.
Why one love grows and one love dies I do not know.
New lovers get drunk on fine wine flavored by bitter wormwood.
We became lovers in the night.
Flowers die to bloom again in another spring.
I want you forever to bloom for me.

Perhaps you have thought of leaving me.
I have such fear in the morn.
I am too much of winter, and too past of spring.
I will not leave you, this I know.
I fear your leaving me in the night.
You are the spring that flowers my mountain wood.

If you should ever leave me, this you must know –
Whether you take your leave in morn or in night –
A spring will flower never more, around one old mountain wood.

Old Words

A child of patience is no child at all.
No child grown old should disagree.
We all must stumble before we can fall.
If you live in chains, you cannot die free.
It is easy we forget the wisdom of youth.
Old hearts like to preach about the grave.
Young hearts get drunk on gin and vermouth.
The old saviors need some young souls to save.
I know, I know – the old like to tell us.
Young love in the morning, young love at night.
They say hearts break – and we know they're jealous.
Still – old folks can be sweet – if you treat 'em just right.

So save these words for when and if you grow dumb.
But these words are wasted on the wise and the young.

A Poet's Prayer

Let us converse in life's poetic line.
And travel the days of life's back highways.
To look for all the rhymes we left in time.
And speak in words deserving of our praise.
Perhaps God gave us our nights and our days.
Perhaps God made the heaven and the hell.
But words we made should never go away.
Our God must know of everything we tell.
If not, then there can be no grace from which we fell.

Love Words Remain

Love's the oldest line in the rhyme of time.
Her music was country and mine was rap.
We loved them love songs lovers make with rhyme.
We both liked rhythm we could tap, tap, tap.
We were rhythm and rhyme, caught in love's trap.
We rock and rolled love words we made to say.
Sweet were her lullabies curled in my lap.
There's no taking back what love gives away.
The love words remain when the end comes to love's day.

Sweet Porn

Favor a little ditty?
Something sweet, short and pretty?
Some poetry that's witty?
No thanks – I'll have the titty.

Eve Was Framed

And so we live for what we do not know,
although we do our best to understand.
It is what God forbid we reap and sow.

It was Satan knew the lay of the land.
It was the Master could not conquer all.
It was Satan bit the Master's hand.

Eve should not be blamed for man's fabled fall.
No child of truth should abide in beauty,
when beauty hides the Warden's garden wall.

A Poet's Heart

The hardest part is the human part.
That's the part God gave to you and me.
We were His greatest works of art.
The hardest part is the human part.
Paradise was lost for the gain of a poet's heart.
God's bliss was lost for desire's choice to be.
The hardest part is the human part.
That's the part God gave to you and me.

The Story of Desire

The story of the world is the story of desire.
To get and be got is the poetry of plot.
The world might end in ice, but it was born in fire.
The story of the world is the story of desire.
Desire is the fire burns time's ev'ry hour.
To live is to want, and then to want not.
The story of the world is the story of desire.
To get and be got is the poetry of plot.

Truth Be Heard

There is no God as far as I can see.
Yet others say they've found the light.
Where is the light to shine on me?
I surely know the darkness of the night.
I would settle for Him just to say a word.
A blind man can know the truth, if truth be heard.

Voice

We search for words of truth to speak and how.
Of life and death and love and beauty proud.
And all the truest words our hearts can vow.
And speak silent for all the world out loud.
And know by truth all voices could be heard.
If truth could find a voice for every word.

Heaven Is the Dark Where God Prays for the Light

"There is a crack in everything.
That's how the light gets in."

~ Leonard Cohen, from *Anthem*

No poet's star can shine without God's night.
A star is a world a word set on fire.
Heaven is the dark where God prays for the light.

A rainbow of beauty starts black and white.
A star is a world made out of desire.
No poet's star can shine without God's night.

In the cold black of heaven stars burn bright.
A star is a world no lie could inspire.
Heaven is the dark where God prays for the light.

A star burns beauty's eternal twilight.
A star is a fire that lovers require.
No poet's star can shine without God's night.

A star burns spaces in time's mortal flight.
A star is a fire from time's sacred pyre.
Heaven is the dark where God prays for the light.

Is there a God of the wrong and the right?
A God of stars and death who can take us higher?
No poet's star can shine without God's night.
Heaven is the dark where God prays for the light.

GLOSSARY

This glossary, like all glossaries, is incomplete. All definitions are incomplete. I have tried to give enough definition to enable the reader to enter the verse form of the poem. For more extensive definitions, please go to the references I have listed in the bibliography.

Ballad A poem that tells a story. Usually in quatrains. Usually *abab* or *abcb*. Usually alternating between four-stress and three-stress lines.

Ballade A French verse form in three stanzas, with three rhymes, and an envoi of four lines. An envoi is a short stanza of conclusion at the end of the poem. The envoi was traditionally addressed to a Prince. Each stanza, traditionally seven lines, now usually eight lines in English, and including the envoi, ends with the same line as the last line of the first stanza. The rhyme scheme is *ababbabA, ababbabA, ababbabA, babA*. I read an authority that said the ballade should have eight syllables to a line. I read an authority that made no mention of syllable count per line. I read poems labelled ballades that varied the syllable count per line. My ballade varies the syllable count per line.

Blues "Oh! The blues ain't nothing but a good man feeling bad," from the *Negro Blues,* by Lee Roy "Lasses" White (1888-1949). The classic form is a stanza of three lines rhymed *AAa*. I followed the classic form, except that I repeated the third line in the fourth and final stanza.

Decima The word means tenth in Spanish. This form originated in Spain. The stanzas are in ten lines of rhyming patterns in eight-syllable meter.

Ghazal The ghazal is an Arabic form dating back to the seventh-century. The romantics brought it to English in the nineteenth-century. The traditional ghazal is composed of couplets. The first couplet is to have a word from the second line that rhymes with a word in the first line. Each succeeding couplet is to have a word in the second line, but not the first line, that repeats this rhyme. The first line of the first couplet is to have a refrain which repeats in the second line of each couplet. My ghazal has the refrain, beginning with the second line of the first couplet, not the first line, and does not have the recurring rhyme. Such a ghazal has been called a free verse ghazal, of which there are many. Since my ghazal does not follow the original Arabic form, I have labelled it a variation in the table of contents.

Haiku/Senryu/Senriu The haiku is a three-line poem that originated in Japan. The lines have five, seven, and five syllables, in that order. The classic haiku includes a reference to a season of the year, as does mine. However, my poem also references human nature, which could also allow it to be called a senryu, or senriu.

Hip-hop According to Tracie Morris, "The two main principles to keep in mind when listening to hip-hop are the patterns and intricacies of rhyme and what is called *flow*, the way the words fit with the music or beat. Like rhyme and flow, the effects of the genre push one's ears forward," *An Exaltation of Forms* (223). I tried to stay true enough to the form to meet the form's essential requirements. If not, it can be called a variation on the form.

Kyrielle The words *Kyrie eleison!* in Roman Catholic Mass mean "Lord, have mercy upon us." The verse form Kyrielle is derived from this invocation. The final line of every stanza is to be the same. There is no set length.

Luc Bat The Luc Bat is a Vietnamese verse form. There is no set length, but the form begins with a six-syllable line, and then goes to an eight-syllable line, and then back to six, until the poem ends on an eight-syllable line. The last eight-syllable line end rhymes with the first six-syllable line.

Ottava Rima Eight lines. Rhyming *ababababcc*.

Pantoum A poem in quatrains with no set length. The poem begins and ends with the same line. The second and fourth lines become the first and third lines of the following quatrain, until the final quatrain in which the first and third lines of the first quatrain become the second and fourth lines of the final quatrain, in reverse order. Up until the final quatrain the rhyme scheme is *abab*. The verse form began in Malaysia and then migrated to France. The requirements of the form, as I have given them, are as the form is usually practiced in English.

Petrarchan Sonnet An Italian verse form, of Sicilian origin, with fourteen lines, named after Francesco Petrarca. The first eight lines rhyme *abba-abba* and are called the octave. The following six lines rhyme *cdeedc, ccddee, cddccd*, or *cdccdc*, or *cdecde*. There may be other possibilities as well. I have written two for this collection with different rhyme schemes in the six-line stanzas, *cdccdc* and *cdecde*. Sonnets are contested territory both as to what can legitimately be called a sonnet, and whether the form has been a means for perpetuating racism and patriarchy.

Rhyme Royal A seven-line stanza poem rhyming *ababbcc*. A form first credited to Geoffrey Chaucer for appearing in English.

Rondeau A French verse form of between thirteen and fifteen lines, with a refrain *R*, formed by the first half of the first line, rhyming *R-aabba, aabR, aabbaR*.

Rondeau Redoublé A French verse form of five stanzas, with each line in the first stanza becoming the end line in the next four stanzas, respectively. The first half of the first line is used as a final refrain. The rhyme scheme alternates between stanzas, *abab, baba.* I have varied the meter of the lines. I do not believe this to be a fatal flaw to the form, but, as always in a poetic democracy, readers can decide.

Roundel An English version of a French verse form (rondel), credited to Algernon Swinburne (1837-1909). The first half of the first line is repeated after the first stanza, and after the final stanza. I know of no set length or meter, but I have, for the most part, followed Swinburne's formatting in his poem titled "The Roundel."

Roundelay I know of no specific requirements for this English variation of the French rondelet verse form. The rondelet rhymes *AbAabbA.* My roundelays rhyme *ababab,* and end with the same two-line refrain after each of my four stanzas.

Rondelet As just stated, the rondelet rhymes *AbAabbA.*

Rubai A Persian verse form that rhymes *aaba, ccdc, eefe,* and *ffgf* in my four-stanza version in quatrains. And *aaba, ccdc, eefe, ffgf,* and *hhih,* in my five-stanza version.

Sestina A French verse form credited to Arnaut Daniel in the twelfth century. It has thirty-nine lines. Six stanzas of six lines each, with a concluding envoi of three lines. The end word of each line in the first stanza is repeated as an end word for each line in the next five six-line stanzas, in a specific order of rotation. So, if the last word of each line in the first six-line stanza is represented as ABCDEF, the second stanza becomes FAEBDC, the third stanza becomes CFDABE, the fourth stanza becomes ECBFAD, the fifth stanza becomes DEACFB, and the sixth stanza becomes BDFECA. The three line concluding envoi must include all the six end words in the following order: the second and fifth words in the first line, the fourth and third words in the second line, and the sixth and first words in the third and concluding line of the envoi, and the concluding line of the poem. That is: BE/DC/FA. My sestina uses the same end syllable for one of the six end words, although the words containing this end syllable sometimes differ when formed as compound words of more than one syllable. I hope that is not too confusing, or a disqualifying rule breaker for claiming to have followed the form.

Shakespearian Sonnet The Shakespearian sonnet, named after William Shakespeare, adopted a rhyme scheme different from the Petrarchan sonnet, and a different stanza form. The rhyme scheme is *abab cdcd efeg gg.* The stanza form is twelve lines and a concluding couplet.

Spenserian Stanza Developed by Edmund Spenser. Nine lines of *ababbcbcc*, usually eight lines of iambic pentameter followed by one line of iambic alexandrine.

Tanaga A Filipino form of four seven-syllable lines, rhyming *aaaa*. Variations in English have also been written *abab*, or *aabb*, or *abba*.

Terza Rima Terza rima is an Italian form meaning third rhyme. It is a three-line stanza. The rhyme scheme is *aba, bcb, cdc*, etc. My favorite terza rima is Robert Frost's *Acquainted with the Night*. Mr. Frost's poem is also a form of the sonnet.

Triolet A French verse form of eight lines, invented in the thirteenth century, with a rhyme scheme of *ABaAabAB*. The first two lines are repeated at the end, and the first line also repeats in the fourth line.

Venus and Adonis Stanza A six-line stanza form, usually in iambic pentameter. Named after Shakespeare's *Venus and Adonis*. It rhymes *ababcc*.

Villanelle An Italian verse form beginning in the sixteenth century. It has five three-line stanzas, and a final four-line stanza. The first line of the first stanza is used as the last line of the second and fourth stanzas. The last line of the first stanza is used as the last line of the third, fifth, and sixth stanzas. The last two lines of the final stanza are the same as the first and last lines of the first stanza, in that order. The rhyme scheme is *aba*. This is the classic form, best represented by Dylan Thomas's *Do Not Go Gentle into That Good Night*. However, poets have created variations. One variation that has gotten a lot of respect is *One Art,* by Elizabeth Bishop.

BIBLIOGRAPHY

Ali, Agha Shahid. *Ravishing Disunities: Real Ghazals in English*. Middletown, CT: Wesleyan University Press, 2000.

Ali, Agha Shahid. *Call Me Ishmael Tonight*. New York: W.W. Norton & Company, Inc., 2003. Professor Ali died on December 8, 2001.[1]

Finch, Annie, and Alexandra Oliver, eds. *Measure for Measure*. New York: Alfred A. Knopf, 2015.

Finch, Annie, and Marie-Elizabeth Mali, eds. *Villanelles*. New York: Alfred A. Knopf, 2012.

Finch, Annie, and Kathrine Varnes, eds. *An Exaltation of Forms*. Ann Arbor, MI: The University of Michigan Press, 2002.

Fry, Stephen. *The Ode Less Travelled*. New York: Penguin, 2005.

Hass, Robert. *A Little Book on Form*. New York: HarperCollins, 2017.

Hirsch, Edward. *A Poet's Glossary*. New York: Houghton Mifflin Harcourt, 2014.

Nester, Daniel, ed. *The Incredible Sestina Anthology*. Austin, TX: Write Bloody Publishing, 2013.

Strand, Mark, and Eavan Boland, eds. *The Making of A Poem*. New York: W.W. Norton & Company, 2000.

---

[1] Professor Ali wrote most of the ghazals in this collection while he was being treated for brain cancer. The first poem in the book is titled, *I Have Loved*: "I must go back briefly to a place I have loved / to tell you those you will efface I have loved."

Made in the USA
Monee, IL
31 October 2020